SMOOTH MOVES

The Relocation Guide for
Families on the Move

Ellen Carlisle

Library of Congress Catalog Card Number: 98-88433

Carlisle, Ellen

    The relocation guide for families on the move.

    ISBN 0-9667827-0-4

Edited by: Ms. Mary Kosmal, Ms. Cindy Bratton, and Mr. Rick Pechstein

Published by Teacup Press
Cover design by Robert Aulicino
Printed by Data Reproductions

This book is available at special discounts for bulk purchases by corporations, institutions, and other organizations. For more information, please contact Teacup Press, P. O. Box 21212, Charlotte, NC 28277. For ordering information, see order forms in the back of the book, or contact Teacup Press directly.

Many thanks to Kevin, Casey, Madalyn, and Allison.

C O N T E N T S

INTRODUCTION

Twenty-two percent of the United States population moves each year. Yes, American families are on the move. Whether you are buying up or downsizing, moving across the street or across the country, moving is an exciting, cumbersome, emotional process. We get better with practice, but who wants practice? When children are involved, a whole new dimension is added, and there is no time for rehearsal. That is why this book is directed to the parents involved when a moving van is required to get from one rung on the corporate ladder to the next. Because let's face it, a smooth move relies primarily on you, Mom and/or Dad. Hopefully, this step-by-step guide will lighten the load and ease the family's transition.

If approached with optimism and a sense of adventure, relocating can provide many advantages. We have been fortunate enough to live in some beautiful places we may not have even seen otherwise. Our eyes have been opened to different ways of living and different types of people. We have made and continue to maintain friendships with people all over the country. As a family we have learned to rely on each other for friendship and comfort, and I expect those bonds to only strengthen over time.

We unpacked from our eighth move and then celebrated our seventeenth anniversary. I am thankful for each relocation, every opportunity. Our children are currently in grades three, seven, and nine, and while they are unique individuals, they represent many generalizations as well. Just keep in mind that within the first year, you will settle into your new post, the kids will establish themselves, and not only will you get from Point A to Point B without a map, you will do so with new friends.

So get out of bed and plaster that smile on your face. A smooth move can have a bumpy start.

So many places,
too little time.
All the strangers' faces
soon to be friends of mine.

Skylines to learn
landscapes to walk
new leaves to turn
different ways to talk.

Find strength within your fear.
Open your mind to the chance
while boosting your career,
your life may be enhanced.

Chapter 1

WE'VE DECIDED TO MOVE--NOW WHAT?!!

When to Tell the Kids

Communication is a wonderful thing but only when timed appropriately. The children do not need to be involved in every decision you and your spouse make on behalf of the family. When relocation is necessary because of a new job or promotion, they should not be aware of every clandestine interview. Children worry, no matter what their age, and chances are the tension is already thick enough. Tell the kids when the offer is imminent. Set up the conversation by pointing out why the current situation has been unpleasant or why a promotion would prove rewarding for everyone.

Highlight all the benefits of the new job. The more these benefits can relate to the child, the better, i.e. a shorter commute will allow for more family time, an increase in pay could provide those long-awaited music lessons. Then when the offer is presented, the child or children will feel as though they are part of the team, an important part of the decision. This inclusiveness is the foundation for a smooth move.

1

Be Prepared

Their initial reaction may be excited, unfazed, miserable, or everything in between. Younger siblings may just look to the oldest to see how they "should" react. If you have never moved before, fear of the unknown can play a large part in the reaction. Some children may withdraw and not want to talk about their feelings regarding the move, especially the teenagers. This only accentuates the negative. Do your best to bring the child into the open with his thoughts, regardless of age.

Allow them their feelings; understand their reluctance to leave friends and familiar surroundings. Show them you have misgivings as well. Let them know that while you are sad about leaving people behind, you are eager to meet new people and make more friends. Reassure them what they are feeling is natural and that you are experiencing the same emotions they are. This will make aligning themselves with you easier, which is essential in team building. Your family is a team, and you will experience this adventure together. Remain upbeat and optimistic; eventually the children will take your cue.

Spreading the News

Once the decision to move is reached, sit down together and discuss how you, as a family, will proceed. You may want to first share the news with family and friends. This initial step can be tough but needs to be done within a few days' time. Word travels fast, and people would rather hear this type of news directly from you than through the grapevine. Encourage the children to tell their friends themselves, but if they really feel they can't, call the parents and ask them to pass the word along. This gives you a chance to explain how your child is dealing with the situation and enlist their child's help and support.

Keeping your children feeling rooted and connected throughout the transition stage is very important. Some children tend to cut themselves off immediately, requiring your focused attention to get them through that difficult time. Keep the communication lines wide open, and do not hesitate to talk directly to your child's friend. An open discussion about how everyone is feeling can be very helpful. Explain that your child may be feeling sad and scared and is especially needy of a good friend's support.

End all conversations regarding the move on an optimistic note. Frequently remind the children why you are looking forward to your new location. Every cloud has a silver lining. For the sake of family harmony, find your silver lining, quickly, and harp on it. (Even if you must practice this in the mirror!)

Chapter 2

SELLING THE HOUSE

Note the use of the word "house" instead of "home."
Now is the time to begin thinking of your house as an article for
sale, a business investment. Try to detach yourself emotionally
so you can view the selling process objectively. "Love makes a
house a home" and "Home is where the heart is." Get through
this business transaction, and turn your next investment into a
home.

First Impressions

First impressions mean a lot to a prospective buyer.
Even before the Realtor is called, give the house a desirable first
impression. Clean out closets, straighten the basement and
storage areas, and fix that dripping faucet--it's time to take care
of all those irritating little projects. The Realtor would just
come in and tell you to do the same, so you might as well take
the time to make the house look great before the Realtor arrives.
Because first impressions mean a lot to the Realtor as well, and
that is the first person you want to impress.

5

Ask a friend whose decorating expertise you admire to look at your home with an unbiased eye. Walk through your home with her/him and try to imagine yourself seeing the house for the first time. Sometimes simple things like rearranging the furniture or grouping wall hangings can transform a room from awkward to inviting. Even though all the furnishings will be removed, tasteful decorating does help sell a home. Only the seasoned buyer can look past the decorating or current "feel" of the home. So make your home feel great! Most people favor a bright home, especially the kitchen. Replace low wattage bulbs in key areas such as the kitchen and bathrooms with 100-watt bulbs. Once you have made your home uncluttered, clean, and bright, it's time to call the Realtor.

Choosing a Realtor

Call at least three realty offices if possible and tell them you are interested in listing your home. They will want to know where you are located, the size of your lot, the size of your home, your school district, etc. Set up an appointment for a Realtor from each office to come to your home. Walk through your home with each Realtor, allowing him/her to become thoroughly familiar with all its features. Solicit suggestions from each one on how to make the house more salable. The more qualified input you can get, the better.

Be prepared to fill out a property disclosure sheet. On this form list any known defects in the house and also any repairs you have made or know have been made to the house. Generally, the seller will be asked to make repairs. Failure to reveal known defects up front on the disclosure sheet could lay the groundwork for legal headaches later.

The Realtor should either have on hand or make arrangements to provide you with "comps," or comparable listings. A comp is a report detailing the description of a specific house for sale. A comp outlines the size of the home, how many bedrooms, bathrooms, garages, what type of heat, water source, exterior construction, floor coverings and amenities of that particular home.

Deciding on your selling price is an important process, and looking at comps is necessary. Review all available comps for current listings as well as recent sales. The recent sales will show you what is selling in your area and the listings will show your competition. They will also highlight the difference between the asking price and the reality of the selling price. If you are in a hurry to sell, you may want to list your house closer to your comparables' selling prices. If you have the luxury of time, you may want to initially try for a higher selling price. Allow yourselves plenty of time to digest this information from all three Realtors before deciding on a price.

Also use this initial time to evaluate each Realtor's handling of your business thus far. You are given a glimpse at their work ethic. Is he/she organized, punctual, eager to win your business? Did your personalities click? Pros and cons only magnify once the process is in full swing.

Deciding on a price and deciding on a Realtor are

different issues. Choose both the price and the Realtor you feel comfortable with, and trust your instinct. A slick Realtor may try to woo the contract by suggesting an inflated price, only to suggest you lower the price a month into the selling process. Choose the Realtor who is genuinely enthusiastic about your home. Realtors who are extremely organized, efficient, and take their business seriously provide the best results. They are handling your most expensive asset. Make sure you are confident in their abilities.

The Selling Contract

Understand your contract before you sign it. Some areas have regulations about the buying agent versus the selling agent and appropriate commissions. Any money you are to be paying from the sale of the house should be satisfactorily spelled out for you.

Decide what items in the house stay with the house, which will be going with you, and which are negotiable. Specify each item in writing in the contract. In many areas anything that is bolted down or adhered to the wall or floor is assumed to be staying unless otherwise specified. But these rules can vary from state to state, so I caution you to become familiar with the rules for your state. For example, if you want to keep the matching curtains to your bedspread or if you want to keep all the curtains in the house, write that in the contract. If you plan to dig up that sentimental shrub you planted when your first child was born, specify that in the contract. If you paid too much money for the dining room chandelier and do not want to just include it in the price of the home, either specify it as "negotiable" in the contract, or replace it and sell it via another means.

Usually realty contracts encompass a three-month time limit, which you have the option to renew. The general feeling is a salable house will certainly sell in that time, however, don't get discouraged if this does not hold true for you. So many factors influence the sale of a house--location, time of year, weather, competition, interest rates, local economy. The three-month contract seems to keep the Realtor trying hard to sell the house while they have the chance. After the contract expires, you are free to renew for another three months, renew on a month-to-month basis, or choose another firm if not satisfied with their efforts in general.

Showings

Realtor Open House

If you live in a densely populated area where competition is keen, your Realtor will, most likely, host a Realtor Open House at your home so that other Realtors in your area can become familiar with your home and will, in turn, keep it in mind when with clients. Generally, the Realtors literally run through your home, absorbing the major details. Do your best to slow them down enough to notice the home's appeal.

Before your Realtor ever shows your home, walk through your home with him/her to familiarize them with the highlights and extras throughout the home. When showing your home, the Realtor should appear knowledgeable about the house; seemingly take pride in the home. A little bit of confidence on his/her part will do a lot to encourage a prospective buyer, which you will understand when you are hunting in the new location.

Open House

A general open house, meaning opening the house to whoever wants to wander through it usually on a Sunday afternoon, is another option to consider. We have been advised to offer open houses and have also been told an open house never sells the house.

Based on our experience, I advise against allowing a general open house unless the competition is so great that you need to encourage traffic into your home. Keep in mind, the attendees can be predominately people looking for decorating tips rather than bona fide buyers. However, if your Realtor is pushing an open house, do consider it. Ad placement is costly as is the Realtor's time spent physically planting himself/herself at the house for those precious weekend hours. Your Realtor must feel very confident about potential results if he/she is urging you to allow an open house.

Appointments

When a Realtor calls to set up a time to show your house, be as flexible as possible. Be prepared to show the house on a moment's notice as well, which means *be neat*. This is easier said than done when you have children, so you must stay on top of the clutter.

Whenever possible, arrange to be out of the house before the Realtor and client arrive. The client will then feel uninhibited while considering your home. Remember, first impressions mean the most, so take special care to make them great. Turn on the lights in the key areas, adjust the temperature for comfort, even simmer cinnamon sticks or brew coffee, if you are available. If you are not available, perhaps your Realtor can arrange to be at your home before the client to turn on lights and light a scented candle. Make your home scream "welcome!" when a prospective buyer walks through the door. Ask your Realtor to turn the lights off before leaving your house if you are concerned about your electric bill!

If you happen to be selling your house during the time of year when the grounds are less than beautiful, leave photos on display of the house surrounded in spring blossoms or beautiful greenery. Choose photographs that highlight the landscaping, not your family enjoying the yard. Allow the prospective buyers to imagine their own family living there.

"We're in your driveway, can we come in?"

When kids are involved, striking a balance between keeping the house clean and ready to show and keeping the kids feeling connected can be tough. You want them to continue inviting friends over to play, more importantly, you want them to continue feeling comfortable enough to do so. If caught off guard by an unannounced showing, simply hustle the kids to the playroom or back yard and remain either in the house or outside with the children while the prospective buyers wander with the Realtor. That "lived in" look and a house full of kids may act as a plus if the buyer is looking for a neighborhood full of playmates for his/her children. If they are interested, a second showing will be arranged. You will be well prepared and forewarned for that one!

The key is to stay calm about house showings, announced or otherwise. Do your best to make the house feel inviting and clean and concentrate more so on keeping the kids happy. The house sale process often drags on for longer than hoped, so everyone will benefit if selling the house is not the focal point of life currently. Anxiety over showing and selling the house can easily translate in a child's mind to doom and gloom. If you are always upset or nervous about the condition of the house or the process of selling, the child may think this is the tone for the entire move. "Remain optimistic"--your daily mantra!

12

Feedback

Maintain a relationship with your Realtor by talking routinely at comfortable intervals. Do not ask your Realtor for follow-up reactions from every showing. You don't want to annoy your Realtor, and frankly, you do not need to hear every single reaction. Back off and let it happen. You have other things to focus on, and your Realtor, most likely, has other houses to sell.

Do tell your Realtor you want to be aware of negatives cited <u>consistently</u>. For example, if nine of ten clients mention an awful cat smell, consider cleaning the carpets. "If you can smell it, we can't sell it," is one Realtor's saying. If the hideous hall wallpaper is a common complaint, you may want to repaper or paint the hallway. A little money invested to sell the house will seem insignificant once the sale is complete and you are free to buy another home in your new location.

A neighbor's house is currently up for sale and remains for sale even though the price has been lowered substantially while other homes in the area are selling. The consistent complaint is that the house is dark. The cabinets are dark, the moldings are dark, the general impression is depressing. In this situation instead of lowering the price, I recommend taking a fraction of that difference and paying someone to paint all the moldings and trim a pleasing shade of white to lighten up key areas such as the entry and living room. It is amazing how much a home will brighten up as a result of lightening up simply the moldings and trim. If things still seem dark, consult a painting expert for advice on lightening or whitewashing the cabinets, walls, and even painted or stained floors. The alternative, for this particular family anyway, is the family's living separately for an undetermined amount of time.

Keep Track

Each time a Realtor shows your house, he/she will leave their business card as a way of letting you know they indeed were there. You can also use these cards to evaluate how frequently your home is being shown and by whom. You may realize another realty agency is actually showing your house more often than the one you have hired, or you may feel reassured that you have made the right choice. Showings do not tell the whole story. Your listing agent acts behind the scenes as well, advertising your home and spreading the news about your listing to other agents. To thoroughly evaluate your Realtor, remember to check the less visible efforts as well.

Keep this information in mind when the time elapses on your current contract. Remember that although a lot of activity is great, only one buyer is needed. That special person is out there somewhere! Once that happens, your Realtor will help you with all the details--contracts, inspection results, and the closing.

Chapter 3

THE HOUSE HUNT

Choosing a Realtor

Once the selling process for your existing home is under way, it is time to think seriously about buying a home in your new location. Arranging for a Realtor to sell your existing home should be relatively easy. However, choosing a Realtor on the buying end can require a bit more work, particularly if you are unfamiliar with the new area.

As with any other service, a recommendation is always best, and hopefully, your employer will provide that. If so, use them! The company's in-house relocation department or recommended relocation company can recommend the best agents, and is also free to discuss areas and school districts frankly. Fair housing laws prohibit the listing agent from steering the client, so frank discussions of areas, etc. cannot be as thorough.

If you are on your own, many chains have offices throughout the country and beyond, so starting with a well-known outfit is your best bet. Get the newspaper from your future area and review the homes for sale. Which realty office lists the most homes in your price range or in your intended area? Going with an agency that does a large volume is a great place to start. You can call ahead and talk to the office manager to get a feel for the office. Ask what a typical yearly volume amount would be for their office. Tell the manager you are shopping around for a realty office, and let them sell you on their office. They should be very willing to win you over with information, and will send you loads of it. Use the realty office as a resource.

You will be spending a lot of time with your Realtor, both in person and on the phone, so getting along well is essential. You should feel comfortable enough with your Realtor to allow him or her to get to know you, your likes and dislikes, so a perfect match can be made between buyer and home. Interview them over the phone before choosing one, and do not ever be afraid to switch agents if the situation is not going well. After all, you are preparing to make perhaps the most expensive purchase of your life!

Being an effective Realtor involves more that just showing houses. Realtors stay up to date about where the best interest rates can be obtained, builder reputations, changing real estate regulations, school district ratings, and proposed developmental changes throughout the area, just to name a few. Do not hesitate to ask questions, and be careful to separate fact from personal preference.

Often your Realtor will act on your behalf when distance prohibits your being there for every little decision. For instance, the sellers of our home wanted to take the runner off the front stairs and needed to replace the runner with carpet. Our Realtor was kind enough to oversee the carpet selection and installation for us because we lived a plane ride away. In general, you will be talking with your Realtor nearly every day, so an amiable working relationship is very important.

Do Your Homework

The more information you can provide your Realtor about your ideal new home situation, the better the Realtor can serve you. Before a Realtor can begin to help you, you and your spouse need to discuss:

How much you are willing to spend?

By now you have determined the selling price of your house and have a good idea of how much equity that sale will net you. Because Realtors tend to show you what is just beyond your comfortable reach, deflate the suggested amount by about 10%. Give the Realtor a range, and then when you do get together, ask to see other ranges for comparison. This helps to solidify the choice you have made, or to reconsider the range you have set.

Be sure to factor in current interest rates when figuring your monthly mortgage payment. If the rates have dropped, you may be able to afford a more expensive home for close to the same payments made under higher rates. A drop of as little as one-half percent can make a significant difference in your monthly payments. Taxes and homeowners' insurance can be paid by the mortgage company directly. If you opt for this, remember to add the estimated amount into your anticipated monthly mortgage payment. Paying on taxes and insurance year-round avoids those large payments quarterly or semi-annually. Call the mortgage broker you plan to eventually use for help in figuring your monthly payments. Perhaps your current loan officer would be amenable to helping you as a courtesy.

Get a map of your future area

AAA, your realty office, or the Chamber of Commerce can provide you with maps. Pinpoint the office or workplace and draw a circle representing an acceptable commuting distance. If you or your spouse spend much of the time traveling by plane, consider using the airport as the circle's center. Refer to this limited area when initially talking with your Realtor.

School district ratings dictate property values

The highest property values are generally found within the best school districts. Let your Realtor know you want to live in the best or second best school district, even if your children are in college or not yet school-aged. When it comes time to sell the house, you will benefit from being in the better school districts. Periodically, the local newspaper will print the scholastic standings of at least a sampling of schools. Public schools are rated on a nation-wide basis as well. Ask your Realtor to provide you with this information.

Ask about available private schools also. You may find them more affordable than you had imagined and/or better geared to your child. Being aware of all your options is a good rule of thumb.

What style home do you prefer?

How many bedrooms does your family require currently and in the future? Which features are important to you--such as, a large kitchen or family room, a level lot, a convenient location? And what don't you like? Think of your existing home and the things you would love to change. Here is your chance! Keep your requirements limited; do not set criteria too narrow to fulfill. Having an open mind can work only to your benefit. Situations may be out there that you have never thought of that would enhance day-to-day life.

In what condition would you prefer your home?

Would you like a brand new home, relatively new, a
home in need of updating, or a true fixer-upper? Are you handy
enough to do many repairs yourself, thereby standing a greater
chance of making money when the house is eventually sold?
Your intended length of stay plays a big factor when considering
the ideal house. A *relatively* new home will probably require less
time and money spent on the house itself than any other option,
especially if the decorating is to your liking. Don't be fooled.
A brand new home is a blank slate, and filling it can be costly.
You will need to decorate, add window treatments, etc. Also a
new house comes with kinks, and they can take time and loads
of effort to work out.

Does your Realtor know your children's ages?

The best welcome in the world is offered by a child your
child's age. The faster your child finds friends in the neighborhood, the faster he will adjust to the move.

Resale

Currently, this may look like a dirty word, but you will
learn to appreciate its meaning. If this is your first move of

many, resale may be perhaps your most important criterion. In order to have a smooth selling process next time around, you need to *buy* right this time, especially if you hope to make money in the process. If resale is your goal, my general advice is choosing a neighborhood with a terrific reputation in a convenient location and great schools. Make sure the builder is/was reputable, and never buy the biggest house in that neighborhood because it cannot appreciate as easily as the smaller ones.

The Initial Visit

After you and your Realtor develop an understanding over the phone and you have digested some of the information you have been sent, it is time for a look around, if possible. Try to make this initial trip without the kids, particularly if they are toddlers. The first look around can be overwhelming and emotional. Narrow down the neighborhoods and get a feel for the area. While you are there, plan a fun itinerary for your first trip as a family. Avoid that "blind leading the blind" anxious feeling when they are with you by familiarizing yourself with the area and getting your bearings straight.

Visit the top-ranked schools

Call the school office, and tell the receptionist you would like to tour the school and obtain the curriculum guide for related grades. She will let you know the best time of day to come and will arrange for a tour guide. Arrive a little early and linger in the hall, noticing the general attitude of the teachers and students. *Take inventory of what the kids are wearing.* This may seem insignificant to you, but to your child, this is very important. Every child wants to fit in, and the easiest way to initially do that is to look the part.

Make an appointment with the principal or assistant principal. Topics for discussion include:

- *How much does the community spend per child?*

- *What is the typical class size?*

- *How much parental involvement does the school enjoy?*

- *What are the educational requirements for teachers and the rate of teacher turnover?*

- *What makes the principal proud to head up that school?*

- *Are before- and after-school care available?*

- *What extracurricular activities are encouraged and how are they supervised?*

- *Just how far in front is the school and why?*

- *What is the routine course of discipline?*

- *Is guidance help available when necessary?*

Take notes and share your findings with your children, enthusiastically, of course.

Taking the extra necessary steps to make you feel comfortable is the key. You need to do everything possible to feel good about the move so you can, in turn, pass this attitude along to your children. Attitude is everything, and yours, Mom and Dad, carry the most influence!

Take photos

Show the children the general landscape. Think of what *you* are wondering about or nervous about, and chances are they are doing the same. Bring home the "Living" or "Entertainment" section of the newspaper, illustrating activities and attractions there. Eliminating the unknown, even bit by bit, helps ease the tension for the kids. Most importantly, bring home loads of enthusiasm and optimism for life in your new location.

The Chamber of Commerce is wonderful. The people there will provide you with information on everything from parks to shopping to upcoming events. Call the Chamber, and they will send you valuable literature. Hopefully, there will be something to spark everyone's interest.

Chapter 4

CHOOSING A NEIGHBORHOOD

House-hunting as a Family

Perhaps you and your spouse were lucky enough to find a home on the initial trip. If a second trip is required, and you can take the children, you will need to prepare them. You will all be spending a lot of time in the car, traveling from house to house, neighborhood to neighborhood, and this gets *really* boring for a child of any age. Provide them with quiet car toys and lots of snacks and be sure to reward them at the end of the day. Take that opportunity to have fun and raise the excitement level. You want them to remember their trip favorably.

Do not demand or expect a favorable reaction on their first visit, the child will likely feel the pressure you are putting on him. Better to watch your own behavior because chances are good the children will follow your lead. Even if the child/children show no enthusiasm and are quiet and antisocial, pay a lot of attention to the positives around you and little to the child's disposition. Full speed ahead! This is the perfect chance to visit the local shopping mall, park, or anywhere kids tend to gather. This will enable your children to see what the kids their ages are wearing, their hairstyles, and how they are behaving. Your older children can measure themselves against the unsuspecting audience and evaluate what is necessary to fit in, at least on the surface.

Finding a neighborhood with children for your children can be easy. Drive throughout the streets slowly with eyes wide open, peering into the backyards. If your children are under seven, look for "rug rat" toys like Little Tikes slides, cozy coupes, jungle gyms, training wheels--snowmen and sleds if the ground is snow-covered. Wooden swing sets and roller blades usually are indicative of the ten and under crowd, while a basketball hoop at regulation height is a sure sign of a boy or girl approaching adolescence. Bicycles of any size are a welcomed sight; especially when there is a pile of bicycles in the driveway. If that's the case, you may want to ring that doorbell and ask what life in that neighborhood is like from a family point of view. A third car can signal a young driver (gasp!) and potential baby sitter (ah!).

If the children are with you, listen to their opinions about the various neighborhoods, briefly discuss their likes and dislikes, and keep them in mind when making your decision. Let them tour the homes with you, and consider their opinions there as well. "This can be my room!" can be heartwarming to hear at this stage. But the actual choice is for the *parents* to make. You want your child to be happy, and you know best how to accomplish that. Making a decision to buy a home is emotional and expensive. A child cannot possibly weigh all the factors, would never consider resale, and has a limited view of the situation, regardless of age.

Honestly, children are happy anywhere that their family, toys, personal comforts, and friends are. We once packed nearly everything we owned into storage and rented a furnished apartment. It was hideous, probably the ugliest furniture I had ever seen, and TINY. Plus I should mention it was located in the dreariest part of upstate New York, and we had left sunny California to be there . . . in January! We had traded a backyard pool for a blanket of snow. My son was two, and I was worried about his reaction. As soon as he saw his toy chest, he was completely at home, never skipped a beat.

How you present your decision, however, can make a world of difference. "We agree with your thoughts on . . ." "You are right about that one house because . . ." "I'm so glad you pointed out . . ." Let them know their opinions matter and do carry weight in the decision process. Make them feel part of the decision, but do not let them dictate it. **DO NOT** allow guilt to play an overriding part in the choice. Buy the home you know is right for your family and your situation.

You Have Found a Home--MAYBE

You think you have found a home your family will enjoy living in for years to come. If relocation will/has become a way of life, you have found a home you can easily sell within

27

a few years. The house meets all your basic requirements and then some. Now the work begins. Evaluate the neighborhood for playmates for your kids. If the rug rat toy search proves inconclusive or you just would like more proof, park your car or sit on the curb near the school bus stop at the appropriate time in the afternoon. Watch the children getting off the bus and again, take notice of their clothing and hairstyles. Keep in mind this may not represent fully the children of the neighborhood, but it will give you a good idea. A fair number may attend private schools, and senior high students do NOT ride the bus, but they are easily recognized driving (speeding) past you.

Do not hesitate to ring doorbells to meet your future neighbors! Of course your teenagers will want to hide on the floor of the car while you do this. Ask potential neighbors why they like living there. Tell them you are considering buying the (current owner's) house and watch their reaction. They may know a dark secret you would like to be in on, or they may be genuinely enthusiastic. Ask about neighborhood activities and their general impressions of living there. If talking freely to strangers seems difficult for them, ask them to steer you to another neighbor who might not mind a brief "quiz" on the neighborhood. As with anything, one person's opinion should not carry too much weight. Talk with as many people as you comfortably can until you feel satisfied with your research.

If you are planning to move every few years, you need to look at your home through relocation eyes regarding purchasing, redecorating and remodeling. Before you purchase the house, you should be reasonably certain:

- *1. The house will sell when you are ready to go, and*

- *2. Any changes/repairs you view as necessary can be made within a timeframe that still allows you to enjoy living there before moving on again.*

Before you put any money into the house, first ask yourself:

- *1. Will this change enhance the house for resale? and*

- *2. Will I likely recoup the money I am about to spend when I sell the house?*

If the answer to both questions is yes, then go for it. If not, put a dollar limit on changes planned just for the sake of changing, list all the changes you would like to make, and prioritize. Divide your list into "musts" and "wants" and, of course, put money into the "musts" first. After they are completed, reevaluate the "wants" and you may deem them unnecessary altogether.

Statistically, kitchen and bathroom renovations can realize up to a 90% return, and landscaping improvements are nearly just as safe. This does not mean change cannot be made simply for the sake of change. Everyone wants to put their own personality into a house, making it their home. And this can be done within every budget, if you plan well and are flexible about desired results. I caution you on the expense involved. Also the time spent on changes inevitably detracts from family time. If you just cannot live with it, change it, but consider the impact as well.

Consider your personal day-to-day time spent in the house and judge accordingly. Of course you will want to decorate the nursery, and you should feel a sense of ownership enough to redecorate anything you want. The children need to feel a sense of ownership of their rooms as well. A fresh coat of paint is well worth the money, time, and effort if it makes your child feel at home and comfortable.

We moved into a house with great potential, and even though the orange animal wallpaper didn't *have* to be changed, I didn't want to live with it either. Instead, we tore it down and painted the room. Paint is a lot less expensive than wallpaper, and a freshly painted room has a great feel. Stenciling and flat faux finishes offer a beautiful, relatively inexpensive effect, and they are easily redecorated. The easy ability to redecorate a home is a plus when shopping for a home, so it can only be an asset in making the home this way. This is an important point to remember when you are not only decorating for yourself but for the next buyers as well. If you do plan to make changes, make them immediately. This will allow you time to enjoy the results of your labor before you move again.

If you are planning to move a lot, and you long to decorate, put your money into furnishings. Keep the walls, carpets, and countertops neutral colors like beiges and whites, and add your personality with accents. You can take furniture, fabrics, and area rugs with you for your next home as opposed to the paint, wallpaper, and wall-to-wall carpeting you will leave behind. This approach allows you to decorate for yourselves rather than for the next owners of your home.

The Offer is Made and Accepted

Your offer should be contingent upon a full inspection of the house, including a building or structural inspection and a termite and insect inspection, if your area of the country is prone to pest problems. *Even brand new homes require a structural inspection.* We had a house built, and the inspector turned up three full pages of items to be attended to or repaired. Think of the situation this way: When you try to sell the home eventually, your buyer will require an inspection, and you will be paying for repairs. Pay the inspector now and the current owner or in the case of a new house, the builder pays for the repairs. If any inspection draws a red flag, you may reconsider buying the house. This contingency lets you out of the contract in such a situation, and at least allows the seller the option to take care of all needed repairs. There may be instances, however, where the buyer and seller agree to share the expense of repair work--such as new carpeting or roofing perhaps.

I recommend you hire your own inspector. After all, you are paying for the inspection, and you can choose whomever you would like. Inspectors are listed in the yellow pages. Also the loan officer you deal with at the bank should be able to recommend a competent one. Of course your Realtor will recommend inspectors as well. Get a few recommendations, talk with each one, and choose an inspector you feel will do the most thorough job. Too often the buyer leaves this choice to someone else to handle because the buyer does not know the area, etc. You do not want any surprises after you move in, and your only chance to avoid those unwanted surprises is if the inspection reveals them first.

Arrange for yourself or your spouse to be present the day the home is being structurally inspected. Do a little inspection of your own and ask the inspector to check out anything that seems remotely questionable. Flush toilets, run water, operate the appliances, the garage door, and the chimney flu. Pick up area rugs to see the condition of the underlying floors, slide sliding doors, open windows, and make sense of every light switch. This is your one opportunity to seek out a deterrent. It always amazes me that everything else you purchase comes with a money-back guarantee. Even the lemon law provides recourse when buying a car. But a house, perhaps the single most expensive purchase of a lifetime, does not come with an equal amount of protection in most states.

Chapter 5

HOME PURCHASE

The Closing

The closing date is determined by the length of time required to process your mortgage loan. Another factor to be considered is the movers' availability. (See Chapter 11.) Before the closing date can be set, arrange for the following:

1. **Mortgage Loan**. Realtors either stay informed themselves on where the best interest rates can be obtained or will refer you to a mortgage broker. You will need to have on hand evidence of your financial worth--such as a pay stub, W-2, monthly investment statements, latest bank statements, a current driver's license. In short, anything that can prove to a loan officer you are worth the financial risk if the bank decides to approve your loan. If your current employment situation is relatively new, bring records from your previous employer.

If you are planning to rent before you buy or your financial papers will be unavailable to you for some reason when the time comes to apply for a loan, consider yourself forewarned. Compile all this information into a file folder or large envelope and keep it in a safe place. A locked drawer at work may be the best spot. The length of time required for processing a loan application varies, but usually you can plan on between four and eight weeks, depending on the type of loan you are securing.

2. **An insurance binder**. A binder is proof of homeowners' fire and hazard insurance, and you are required to present an insurance binder at the closing. Your current insurance agent may have a branch office to tell you about in your new area, or you may want to take this opportunity to shop around for another agency to handle your insurance needs. Home and auto insurance can vary tremendously from state to state, so you may want to do some comparative shopping.

3. **An attorney**. In some states you are required to hire an attorney to handle the closing. The actual transaction usually then takes place at the office of either the buyer's or seller's attorney. Some states do not require an attorney to be involved at all, in which case you may close anywhere. We closed in a hotel lobby in Seattle by handing our loan officer a certified check. The whole transaction was accomplished before our morning coffee. Whether you need a lawyer or not, bring your certified loan check, and your own checkbook. There are always incidental fees to cover.

The Walk Through

Just prior to the scheduled time of closing, you are allowed a Walk Through, if you specified this in the sales contract. This means you literally walk through the home you are about to purchase. If the soon-to-be-former owners have cleared out, you will be walking through an empty house. Prepare yourself--houses once filled look amazingly different when emptied! Look for any damage their movers may have done and make a list to discuss at the closing if necessary. Here again, the rules can vary from state to state, and not all homeowners are required to vacate prior to closing. Never assume the situation will be similar to the one you are leaving, so ask that the process be laid out for you.

When you do take possession or during the walk through, check for anything left behind that should not have been if the home is vacant, and check that items deemed to remain in the house are still there. Check that any repairs deemed necessary by the inspection have been satisfactorily completed. If not, get in touch with your realtor right away. In short, this walk through provides a look at the actual home you are about to buy. Any questions or reservations should be brought up before the closing if possible.

Relocating at a Company's Request

Review all the benefits your employer offers regarding moving, *before* you accept the offer. In this way you will know what you are getting yourselves into before the situation arises. Some companies are better than others, but most will try to lighten the load somehow. In general, companies want to do whatever possible to keep their employees and their families happy, so ask questions. Often a company's moving policy is not clearly defined so that they can bend the rules somewhat when individual and unique situations arise. Ask in advance what the company is willing to do to help with the financial burden.

Chapter 6

BUILDING A HOME

Several factors contribute to the decision to build: The area is booming, and new neighborhoods are everywhere; the market is so slow that nothing is available that suits your needs; you have unique requirements such as a horse paddock; or maybe you have just always dreamed of building your own home.

Before you dive into such a project, consider: Will the family need temporary housing until the house is completed? Will you live in the house long enough to enjoy the fruits of your labor before you move again? Can you afford the finishing costs for decorating, landscaping, etc. within your timeframe?

If you are planning to build a new home in an existing, established neighborhood, the tips on the neighborhood search still apply. However, if your project will be in a brand new neighborhood, more risk is involved. Thoroughly research the facts relating to that area--such as, the school district, proximity to the grocery store and conveniences, how many homes are planned for the neighborhood. Equally important: How will the area surrounding your neighborhood be developed? Imagine spending you first night in your newly constructed home. Now imagine your peaceful sleep interrupted by the snorts of a bulldozer just beyond your backyard border clearing the way for a four-lane road! It can happen. Call the planning director of your city or town, where you can find out what is planned several years down the road.

A wealth of information can be gleaned by reading the by-laws of the development. The by-laws spell out rules regarding everything from lot size, intended house size restraints, property drainage, side or front facing garages; the actual blueprint of the layout including sidewalks, street lamps, common areas, the natural topography--all contribute to a detailed mental picture of the proposed project. Are you able to choose a builder, or are all the lots owned by builders? If so, tour existing homes built by that builder and talk to the homeowners about the builder's work ethic.

When choosing a lot, consider its size, how the house you are intending to build will be situated on the lot, the exposure to the sun, the traffic that will likely be on the street. Have the surrounding lots been sold? What type of home is planned for those lots?

Deciding on a builder requires a bit more work. Do your research! Information on a builder's reputation can be obtained through the HBA or Home Builders' Association and through prior customers. Of course any builder you consider should be thoroughly checked out through the Better Business Bureau.

I strongly urge you to contact as many people as possible, but my favorite resource is the loan officers at various banks. The loan officer disburses the draws from the construction loan with the borrower's OK. If there is a problem between the builder and borrower, you can bet the loan officer will be aware of it. That's not to say a builder with a fine reputation will not sour, or a builder with a somewhat negative reputation will not be trying harder to improve. Get your Realtor involved as well. Not only is he/she likely to have experience in this area, but he/she will act as liaison when necessary. And having someone in your corner during this potentially stressful time is very comforting.

Interview several builders and trust your instinct. Require an extremely detailed contract that leaves little room for interpretation. Make sure the builder understands your expectations room by room, detail by detail. A mutual respect between builder and client is necessary, even if you would not choose him as a friend. Once your choice is made, the builder and loan officer will guide you through the process.

And building a home is a *consuming* process. There is an adage about building a home that advises to be prepared to double the price and double the time. That is not far from the truth. I have yet to meet someone who moved into their new home on the anticipated date and did not pay a whole lot more than originally planned. Beware of Builder Allowances. The builder stipulates allowances for lighting, kitchen appliances, flooring, etc. in the contract. This amount may seem substantial . . . until you try to buy all the lighting for the house for that amount and realize it provides for about half. But knowing to expect delays and overages ahead of time can work to your advantage and help to keep your nerves calm. Delays are inevitable. But if you shop before you sign, allowances can be more realistic.

While we were agonizing over lighting in a store, we met a woman, blueprints in hand, who had come to get an idea of how much money she should plan on spending. She had not even chosen a builder let alone broken ground. The salespeople in these stores can make recommendations for "required" lighting according to room size and desired effect just from looking at your house plans. You can likewise take your plan to shop for faucets, sinks, kitchen appliances, carpeting, etc. By doing so you can know ahead of time just how much money these necessities will cost you. The better you can get a handle on costs for *everything* going into your home, the more prepared you will be to sign a contract for a specified price. If you are not a detail-oriented person before you begin building a home, you will be by completion.

Usually a builder will offer several house plans from which to choose. This is an ideal way to tackle your first attempt at building. You are able to walk through the house rather than just visualize it from a blueprint. Actually feeling the size of each room is such a plus when considering each plan. Any changes you would like to suggest can be done so concretely--for example, a bay window instead of casement windows, an open foyer instead of a room above. And since the house plan has been built before, the allowances may all be simply built into the price. Often you are given choices for each option--such as, cabinet and floor finishes, carpet color, lighting, exterior construction, etc. If you really want to build and know your time there will be limited, or if you are a first-time builder, I encourage you to find this type of situation. A lot of anxious guesswork is eliminated, hidden costs are more easily identified up front, and completion dates can be more on target.

Some people think building a home means once the task is complete, the work is over. Think again. Once the home is constructed, the big-ticket details remain-- landscaping, window treatments, decorating, furniture. Often the landscaping is part of the contract price, and you may be wise to stipulate that as such. And anticipate working out the kinks that are inevitable in a new home. Leaks, inoperable windows, faulty dishwashers--all these and more are among repairable inconveniences expected in a new home. Definitely hire an independent inspector to inspect your home before you close and certainly before the last disbursement is made to the builder. Dangle this carrot until all repairs are made.

All negatives aside, building a home in a brand new neighborhood can be very rewarding, and a new neighborhood provides a wonderful atmosphere, particularly for the children. New neighborhoods attract families. Perhaps the family is building to accommodate its changing needs or to satisfy particular requirements and preferences. For whatever reason, your children, as newcomers, are among other newcomers as well. Being surrounded by lots of "new kids" is very comforting when you are a new kid yourself. Because everyone is new to the neighborhood, people are usually very eager to meet their neighbors.

Watching your vision of a home appear first on paper then be transformed into an actual structure is thrilling. Being in on the beginnings of a large project provides a sense of ownership and pride, which can be very beneficial to a family new to an area. That pioneering camaraderie is something we are forever grateful to have shared.

Chapter 7

WHEN TO CLOSE

If One Parent Leaves First

Unfortunately, the luxury of choosing our own timetable is not always provided. More often than not, the spouse responsible for the relocation is the first one to go to the new area, and could leave months before the rest of the family. This is not always a bad thing.

As with any new situation, there is a period of adjustment. In my experience, allowing my husband to adjust alone has been best. He is under stress, trying to focus 100% of his attention on the new position, working extra hours, making friends, and settling into the new environment. Sound fun to be with? During this initial adjustment, he is usually too drained to help his needy family emotionally anyway. We have found it best to let him get comfortable first, while we stay comfortably at home. Then when we have made the move, he is better able to extend a helping hand.

If you find yourself in this situation, help the kids develop their compassionate side. They miss their Mom or

Dad, and hopefully, realize the importance of being together. Encourage the children to write letters. This provides your child with the opportunity to express himself on paper, where he may find it easier to reveal his inner thoughts. Allow your child plenty of privacy when writing. You may hear a lot of crumpling papers as he starts over and over. The important part is he is formulating his thoughts. E-mail is a great option if available. It's quick and easy and helps the child develop his keyboarding techniques at the same time.

Many people find writing emotional thoughts much easier than saying them. You just may be surprised at how frank the response is. (And be sure if your child writes to you, he gets a response.)

Plan Ahead

By planning ahead, you will be able to alleviate much of the stress the separation can cause. If you are considering making a move that will involve a separation, negotiate for ways to lighten the load before accepting the position, if possible. Discuss up front and get a clear understanding of how frequently you would like to go home, and that extra time off will be required from time to time. When you have children, special events occur frequently--the first dance recital, musical performance, ball game. Of course we cannot always get what we want, so we must focus on the big picture. If a special event must be missed, fill the void with phone calls, notes of encouragement, etc. Children are amazingly resilient, and the video camera becomes a treasure.

Weekend Visits

As long as Mom/Dad comes home on the weekends, this situation can work well for a few months with children over about ten. But do not be fooled. Just because a child has maturity enough to outwardly behave well in this situation, children of all ages are affected by the absence of a parent. Little ones may cry for the parent while teenagers may just sulk but say nothing is wrong. Younger children seem to be more negatively affected if visits are limited or if the situation continues for too long. Also just the added work heaped on the spouse at home where little children are involved provides too much stress. This situation can deteriorate quickly. Try to limit this situation to weeks instead of months.

A daily phone call is always appreciated. When children under ten are involved, call in the mornings rather than the evening. A chat with a far-away parent is a great way to jump-start the day, providing enthusiasm to get out of bed in anticipation for this special talk time. If the call is put off till the end of the day, the child may be over tired, and the sound of his parent's voice may just make things worse. "Hurry and get to sleep so you can talk in the morning" may become an effective bedtime coax.

Silver Lining

Make good use of this time of separation by planning for the next time you are together as a family. Arrange to have the local paper from your new location delivered to you. If that is not possible, ask your Realtor to send you a copy from time to time. Usually Thursday's paper lists upcoming events, things to do, places to go. Provide concrete evidence for your children that there is "life" where you are going and fun to be had.

This is also a good time to complete that long-awaited project you have been avoiding, such as photo albums, etc. Take time to collect photos of current friends, neighbors, home, and surroundings. Familiar photos will be very comforting when you land in your new area.

Although the workload is heavier during one parent's absence, focusing on the children seems easier. Take advantage of this situation. Connecting with each child individually can provide time to ease anxieties and quell fears. Talk often about the absent spouse and what he/she is doing. As highlights of the new area are discovered, the rest of the family can discuss them and gain some enthusiasm. Make the most of this interim time; turn it to your advantage! Look at the bright side because there always is one.

Chapter 8

THE BEST TIME TO MOVE YOUNG CHILDREN

<u>Pre-K through Grade Five</u>

There are differing opinions about the best time to move a child, and they all have merit. I do believe each child is different, and you need to trust your instinct. However, my experience, coupled with many opinions of parents who have gone through the process, help me to make the following recommendations in order of preference.

As you will see, I definitely recommend moving a child in this age group at varying times during the school year. The most important tip for these children is the "buddy system." Ask the teacher to appoint a child to be your child's buddy for the first week of school. The buddy should be someone well respected by the other classmates, whose opinion carries a lot of weight. This child can show your child around, and hopefully, introduce your child to some friends. Most importantly, the buddy can provide company during lunchtime, which is apparently the hardest part of the day to get through for the newcomer. Often a parent will volunteer to meet the child for lunch, but having mom or dad there is not always the best idea. Get your child's permission rather than planning a surprise visit.

Remember to provide reassurance along the way, regardless of when the move is made and how well the child is doing. Reinforce the positive progress by acknowledging it and commending him accordingly. And of course children of all ages benefit from extra hugs during stressful times. (Don't you?)

Just After the School Year Begins

Anytime *after* the first six to eight weeks of the school year have passed is a great time to move your child, provided of course the child has spent that time in his current school. The new classmates have had time to adjust to their classroom situation, friends, and routine and can then extend themselves to an incoming student. Teachers and students make quite an effort to welcome the "new kid," especially after they feel comfortable enough with their own situations. Your child receives instant recognition, and his classmates have only one new name and face to learn as opposed to the sea of new faces presented just six to eight weeks before.

If your family does leave during the Autumn, you may want to consider going back "home" over the holidays for an emotional boost. However, putting the move off until after the holidays may not be as rewarding as hoped. We made that mistake. The result was the saddest holidays we had ever spent, lamenting over our *last* Thanksgiving, our *last* Christmas, our *last* everything in *this* house. Animosity surged, and you can image how heavily the emotional atmosphere hung when the typical post holiday blues were coupled with packing up our household.

The best option in this situation would be to stay in your new home for the holidays and invite family, former neighbors, old friends and new. This gives the whole family something to look forward to, plan for, and work towards. A reason to hang pictures! The anticipation of company is a wonderful incentive to settle into your new surroundings. Gathering old relationships into your new surroundings has a great housewarming effect. Let the children lead the house tour, enabling them to take pride and ownership.

During Winter Break

Some schools have a break during February, which can be the perfect time to make a move. The holidays have been enjoyed and put away, and the kids can unpack and adjust to the new surroundings without missing school.

Up to Six Weeks before School Ends

Moving anytime during the school year can be beneficial, even this close to the end. Your child has time to learn names and faces and even make friends in this time. He has plenty of time to learn his way around the new school--in short, everything will be familiar after the summer flies by and it is time to return to school. If your child is interested in playing spring and summer sports, you can get him/her there in time to sign up and play. Summer activities and camps may be set up early in the spring as well.

You need to act quickly to help your child establish friendships before the end of the school year. Suggest your child invite friends over after school or on the weekend. Invite classmates for a Friday evening pizza party. Post a sign-up sheet at school for an evening picnic in the park for families, and maybe everyone in your family will make a friend. Save the sign-up sheet with phone numbers for later use. The goal here is to work quickly to help your child feel comfortable enough to call friends over the summer; otherwise, it is going to be a *long* one. The unpacking can wait--this is definitely more important.

If you do plan to move at this time, try to schedule a visit back to the old neighborhood during the summer. This seems to provide that added boost of confidence needed to pursue new friends outside school bounds.

At the Beginning of Summer

Waiting for school to end has merit, but it makes for a long and lonely summer. If your neighborhood has a pool or a common area, or you are able to join a recreation facility, you are in luck. Kids need to have someplace other than home where they belong and where they can be with children their own age. If you must move during the summer, make sure they have a built-in link to friendships. If you do not plan to join a recreation facility, try the local library. The library not only offers story time year round, but there you can scan spring newspaper issues detailing summer camp schedules. Here again the Chamber of Commerce can be a huge help. The YMCA seems to have a branch just about everywhere across the country and that is a wonderful facility for any age. Research what options are available because of your new location, i.e. 4-H in the mid-west and boating instruction on the coasts or lakes.

But even when your child is completely entrenched in a summer routine, the scary thought of the unknown school looms in the not-too-distant future. Offering the ideal start in his new home is far more important than a comfortable end in his old home. And since school is such a large part of your child's life, reaching for the best incoming situation is paramount.

At the End of Summer

The advantage of your child being ready to start his new school on the first day is strictly academic. He will not miss any instruction and will be aware of how things are handled from the start. He will learn with everyone else what is expected of him.

The biggest disadvantage is the lack of time for personal situations--such as, getting to know the neighborhood children, becoming familiar with his new area, and having the chance to feel settled at home before conquering school. Having everything new at once is stressful for any age. He will also be forced to make new acquaintances while learning his way around a new school.

Moving Younger Children

If your children are not yet school aged, you are in luck. You really are not limited to any specific time of year, but the sooner the better if one parent will be absent for a while. Children this age will definitely take their cue from you. If you are unhappy about the move, they will show your unhappiness; if you are excited, they will be as well.

When we were moving and anticipating a time of separation for our two-year-old son, I sought the advice of our pediatrician. He assured me that as long as either Mom or Dad was planning to stay with the child, we had nothing to worry about. Instead he was concerned about who would console poor Dad while separated from our son! Kids can cope with just about anything. Sometimes we want to be missed, and they are more accepting than we hoped!

During the transition time be sure to provide young children with their old comforts. Remember to keep handy that special blanket, favorite toys and books--anything that is comforting and makes the child feel at home wherever he is. Make a photo album of his favorite places, such as the yard, the play area, under his bed. He may not be able to verbalize what he's missing, but he may be able to point to a picture.

When you do arrive, take the children to story time, swimming lessons, the park--anywhere they can be with children their own ages. You may even meet a friend there too. A good friend laughs about "picking up" another mom at McDonald's playground when she first arrived. They have become great friends! Facilities such as the YMCA and some churches provide mom and tot programs and/or drop-in daycare for "mothers' morning out."

Chapter 9

MOVING YOUR TEENAGER

Moving teenagers can involve more difficulty and may require more help. Special care must be taken to ensure a smooth transition. Guidance counselors and experienced parents recommend not moving a child in the eighth grade or older, PERIOD. However, in today's transient society, never say never. So when you do not have the luxury of planning your own timetable, proceed with caution. The following information applies when relocating middle school and high school students.

Your teenager needs to be treated differently than younger siblings from the beginning of the relocation process. Once you have made the decision to relocate, you will need to include your teenager moreso for two reasons: 1) He is probably astute enough to notice his parent's unhappiness and will draw his own conclusions unless told otherwise; and 2) A teenager wants to be treated more like an adult, so including him early on can only enhance your chances of a smooth move.

This is a highly volatile age, so be prepared for some extreme reactions. He may declare life-long hatred for you and insist he will not make the move. At this age the teenager is trying to exert his independence, so treating him like a younger child will only backfire. Be patient, maintain your composure, and keep talking . . . calmly. Allow your child time to come around on his own, just as you would an adult.

Solicit your teenager's help in sharing the news with younger siblings. Convince him to put on a good attitude for the sake of the younger children, thus making him part of the adult team. Let him know you are confident he can behave like an adult and that you are relying on him to do so.

Give your teenager the chance to tell his friends himself. Seeing genuine sadness the news brings to valued friends can bolster confidence in making new ones. A word of caution here: Try to keep the news of the move quiet until close to the time of the actual move. Kids tend to pull back when they hear their friend is leaving, and your child may feel left out at a time when he needs his friends most.

Let your child know he can e-mail, write, or call these friends as often as needed. And be aware that "needed" is the correct word. An adolescent going through puberty is especially needy of close friends for support and co-misery through this often-awkward stage. Until they find the necessary support group in the new location, allow him to benefit from the old group. Let him know you understand his need is real, and the reasons are his alone, no explanation required.

Give your teenager every opportunity to help in the selling process, but do not expect much involvement. View passive objections as a good sign, and any help as a plus. Do expect him to keep his room neat for showings and to pitch in when keeping the common areas neat as well. He may want to remove personal items from view, which is ok. Give and take is good at this time and should be encouraged.

His First Visit

Ideally, you can make the initial trip without your teenager, so that you can plan for his favorable first impression. But try to arrange for his initial visit as soon as possible. Chances are really good he is imagining his new location with negative overtones, to say the least. The sooner you can win him over, the better. So either take a quick trip if possible without him, or during employment-related visits scout out possible neighborhoods and fun spots, then bring him down to "help" make decisions.

Do consider his opinion when choosing a home and a neighborhood, but of course do not let him dictate your decision. Perhaps narrow down the choices and allow him to help choose. You do want your teenager to feel comfortable in the new surroundings and being excited about the new house or area can only benefit the situation. Just knowing his opinion is valuable to you can ease your teenager onto your side in this uprooting adventure. Making him feel a part of the decision is particularly reassuring for the teenager because he wants to feel in control of his life. This control is obviously threatened because he is being forced to relocate. He will be grasping for parts of the process he can control or at least be involved in. Let this involvement work in your favor! Your teenager just may have some great input!

Visit the Prospective Schools

Arrange for a guided tour around the schools you are considering either through choice or geographic boundary. I am assuming you have already done the research into school rankings, etc. What you and your teenager need to observe during this visit are the other children in school. At this tender age, fitting into the new surroundings is extremely important. Teenagers need to dress like the other kids, and to some extend, be like the other kids. Help your child maintain his individuality while making every effort to help your child fit in. Note clothing styles and hairstyles, and take a trip to the mall as soon as time permits. New clothes can help to boost spirits while helping him assimilate.

After the "most important" things are taken care of, gather and assess the following information:

- *Obtain a School Calendar, so you are aware of start and end dates, semester breaks, and grading periods.*

- *Does the school operate on a traditional or block system? Ask for a copy of a student's schedule in the grade your child will be entering.*

- *What are the hours of a school day?*

- *Is the schedule A/B, or is each class offered every day?*

- *What is the goal of the school? Is college prep stressed equally with vocational training? How are students prepared for SATs?*

- *What elective choices are available throughout the high school years?*

- *What sports are offered? Are intramural sports available as well?*

- *What clubs or after school activities are available, and are they well attended?*

- *How does the school inspire camaraderie and spirit among its students?*

- *What is the routine course of discipline? Ask for a student handbook.*

- *What are the educational requirements for the teachers?*

- *Ask what is recommended to ensure your child's feeling comfortable as well as succeeding at that particular school.*

The Best Time to Move your Teenaged Student

When making a move during the middle or high school years, have your student there for the first day of school if at all possible. The beginning of the year is when adjustments are made, parameters are set, and expectations are spelled out.

Assemblies are held by grade. During these assemblies, students learn what the school's expectations are for itself and for its students, "We want to be Number 1 in the system and be known as the most spirited school as well." The student is "introduced" to prominent people in the school--guidance counselors, assistant principals, the principal, and student council leaders.

In the very beginning of the school year, students learn what is expected of them for each teacher. These expectations are clarified through trial and error and illuminated for the whole class to understand as soon as possible.

Some schools have homeroom time at the beginning of the day throughout the year; others eliminate this hand-holding time after the initial few weeks. The extra reassurance this time offers can be very comforting to a student just beginning in the system.

On the personal side, the most beneficial aspect of this shaky initiation is that it lays the best ground for camaraderie. Even if a student is returning for the second or third year, the beginning can still be a good time for making new friends. Often the clubs recruit new members at this time as well, which does not mean a child cannot join later in the year, space permitting. Being there from the start is the ideal situation all around.

Of course the most important aspect to consider is academic. High school systems and schedules can vary from state to state and even school to school within the same state. And most northern schools start two to three weeks later than schools in the south. If a student begins school after Labor Day, is adhering to the block system, and changes schools after three months, the results can be disastrous. If that student then enters a school that had started three weeks earlier and operated on a traditional schedule, he has missed a lot of required instruction. He, most likely, will have to catch up in summer school.

Conversely, if a student arrives towards the end of the school year, the results can be equally disastrous. Regardless of when that student arrives, he will be required to take the final exam or end-of-quarter test. He may be completely unprepared depending on the schedule he had been on in the previous school. And as you are fully aware, all high school grades are reflected on the permanent record.

If you must move during the school year, relocate during the new school's semester break. This will allow the student a fair start to the second half of the year. Arrange for any necessary testing by either school to be done during that break time.

Helping your Teenager Adjust

Encourage your child to join a small group, such as a club, the band, or a sports team. The adjustment, which in his mind is a huge interruption in his life, is more easily tackled bit by bit. Becoming involved in a small group can facilitate his making new friends. In fact, the whole small group may instantly become his new circle of friends, and then he can branch out from there. Anything you can do to help reinforce these friendships can only benefit the entire family. Because parents know an unhappy teenager can make the whole family miserable.

Encourage him/her to have friends over or take a few special recruits to a sports event, show, etc. This initial personal stretch may not come easily. Be patient to a point. You know your child, and you know how long is a sufficient waiting period for shyness, or simply laziness. A little prodding can go a long way. He will be grateful when new friendships are formed, and life can resume as before.

The key is encouragement. Give your teenager as much one-on-one time as possible. Encourage your child to make friends, work hard at school, and get involved in his new school, area, and/or activities. Set an example for your child by getting involved yourself. Perhaps you can join something together to show the way and illustrate how easy adjusting can be. Encourage him, work with him, communicate with him, and play with him. And let him cry on your shoulder along the way if necessary. Good comes from everything, and finding that good together can only enhance your relationship, boost his confidence, and help ease the process for inevitable life changes in the future.

Chapter 10

CLOSURE

Regardless of when you make your move, remember one thing before you go: CLOSURE. Human nature requires completion, a sense of finality. Say good-byes to classmates and teachers, neighbors and friends. Walk door to door if you must. Bid farewell to people in your life who will wonder where you have gone--such as, the favorite cashier at the grocery store, the dry cleaner, your auto mechanic. Give these people a chance to wish you and your family well, while illustrating to them they have made an impact in your life.

Show your children how your lives are enhanced by acquaintances. Good-byes can make for bittersweet endings, but the compassion and parting words can bolster your and your children's confidence in making new relationships. Also, proper good-byes leave the door open to continue relationships from a distance. You never know who will be passing through and how heartwarming a familiar face can be when you have been far from "home."

Make sure your child has something tangible to remember his favorite friends, such as photographs or momentos of some kind. My children cherish their T-shirts signed by all the neighborhood children. They use them for sleeping shirts, and when the children put them on, it's like getting a big group hug. The shirts have provided for cozy, sweet dreams and reassurance, especially in the beginning. Photo albums can include not only smiling faces but favorite rooms, hiding places, forts, trees, pets, and welcoming front doors.

Chapter 11

BEFORE YOU LEAVE

The Movers

A specific moving company may be provided by your employer. Companies who move their employees usually have contracts with specific movers who handle all their moves. If that is the case, consider yourself lucky. Usually the more experienced movers are sent when a contract is involved.

If you are locating your own moving company, get three estimates, and do not sign anything without your employer's OK if they are helping you with the costs. If you are relocating without assistance, do a bit of research on your prospective mover. Call the Better Business Bureau to make sure you are dealing with reputable movers. Obtain letters of recommendation and try to talk with past customers. Remember, you get what you pay for--the cheapest is not always the best choice.

Getting an estimate involves a representative from the moving company physically walking through your home to get an idea of the weight of your possessions and anything requiring special handling, etc. How many cars will your employer pay to move and how will they be transported? If you are paying for the move, is the cost of driving, including hotels, preferable to the mover's transporting your car? Ask about transporting houseplants. Typically, the mover will not insure a plant's safe delivery. Some movers will not even take them on the truck. If you are moving to a citrus state, vegetation of any kind is not permitted over the border for fear of pest infestation. Other definite no-no's include chemicals, propane tanks for the gas grills, aerosol spray cans, and alcohol. Any forbidden item could ruin the entire contents of the truck, or in other words, your every possession. You will want to dispose of them or drive them yourself to your new destination.

Once a mover is chosen, a specific moving date can be arranged according to your ideal closing dates for both houses. The summer remains the busiest time of year to move. If you are planning to close during the summer, give your moving company as much notice as possible so you can be scheduled before they are booked.

New and Old Addresses

Getting the Word Out

You have chosen a new house, and all indications say you will be moving into that home sometime in the near future. You can get your new phone number now by simply calling the phone company in your new area. The phone company will need your new address and move-in date. Ask that the phone be effective for your move-in day. You may want to order pizza, call the movers' office, your office, etc. For the children's sake, request a phone number that is easily remembered, and the phone company will try to oblige.

Compile your new address and phone number and/or e-mail address on a business card, change of address card, sheets of paper, anything, and make sure everyone you would ever want to keep in touch with has a copy. Give your children plenty to pass around to their friends, or better yet, let them make their own. This will help them memorize their new information. Provide your children with a new address book for them to fill with their friends' addresses and phone numbers. Freely give out writing paper and/or printer paper to facilitate their writing to your children.

Your child will benefit from bridging that friendship gap by keeping in touch with old friends until new friendships are formed at least. Hopefully, they will never lose contact with that precious few, but that will require your effort as well. The letters and phone calls will slow to a comfortable level once new friends are made. Correspondence tends to slack off to just a chosen few, which is a good sign when that does occur. In fact, if your child leaves behind a large group of friends, encourage him to choose one or two through whom he can keep in touch with the entire group rather than trying to write to each one individually. The job can be too cumbersome and may be avoided altogether, especially for boys, who can tend to be short on paper conversations.

Change of Address Cards

As soon as you know your new address, phone number, and move-in date, you have some paperwork to take care of. Get yourself a stack of change of address cards at the post office, and while you are there, fill out a forwarding notice. Write your vacate date as the effective date of your new address. Pick up a supply of post card stamps for the address changes too and keep them together, preferably where you sort your mail or write your monthly bills.

As the moving date nears, replenish your supply of change of address cards. Each time something comes in from a company that will need your new address, fill out a change of address card right then and send it off. You may want to keep a running list of companies you have sent address change cards to for your records.

Look through your files for companies you deal with

once or twice a year, such as your accountant or investment companies. Make sure your current employer has your new address, even if you did not change companies. This will help simplify your life at tax time. Previous employers need to be aware of your current address. When it comes time for pensions and benefits, you will want them to know where to find you.

This may be the perfect project to enlist your child's help. Designate an "in-box" for magazines, catalogs, and other mail items, and teach your child to fill out the change of address cards. The more useful the child can be, the more he will feel like part of the group.

Utilities

Gas, electric, telephone companies--all need to be called. Keep your phone service until the day after your intended vacate date. That way if you are delayed a day, you will still be covered. Even on moving day, the phone will come in handy. When terminating your gas and electric services, do not have them disconnected; simply request they terminate service *in your name* the day after your intended vacate date. Reconnecting gas service, for example, can require painstaking, time-consuming steps for the new owners that can easily be avoided.

When talking to the electric company representative, ask about a letter of reference. A letter of reference from your current company indicating you pay your bill on time may help avoid a deposit in your new location. At the same time ask for a refund for any deposits you may have been required to pay when you initially set up service. In all cases, your final bill will be sent to your new address.

Magazines

Clip out the address labels of your magazines, tape them in the "previous address" spot, and fill in your new address in the appropriate place. Many periodicals now have an 800 number you can use when changing your address if you prefer. Magazines generally catch up two or four issues later, so plan accordingly.

Doctors

Tell your family's doctors and dentists you are planning to move. Some doctors will give you ex-rays and files directly; others require you to fill out a form authorizing them to send your information directly to your new doctors.

Clean Out!

As the moving date nears, clean out your freezer, refrigerator, and pantry. Inevitably, food will be left over. Arrange with a neighbor to take the left over perishables if you don't want to throw them away. The nonperishables from your pantry can be packed. If you are moving your refrigerator, empty it completely a day or two before the movers arrive. Tape a box of baking soda to the inside, and leave the door ajar. This will alleviate the nasty odor that will accompany a closed refrigerator. If you plan to leave the refrigerator, make sure it is empty, clean, and the temperature control is on the lowest setting. Turn off the icemaker, if applicable.

Go through your closets, your kids' clothes closets, linen closets, attic, play areas, etc. and clean out the clutter. Get boxes from the supermarket, fill them, and take them to Goodwill, Salvation Army, wherever, or the dump. This exercise may hurt emotionally, but you will be so happy when unpacking only useful, needed items. Imagine not having to devote closet space to junk? After three moves, I had the cleanest closets in town.

The kids can help tremendously while preparing to move. Make sure everyone has a chore. Set aside blocks of time when the whole family is busy getting ready for the move. Even the little ones can empty trashcans and sort their own toys. If everyone is cleaning out, they will be sure to offer something as well. Group efforts do a lot to inspire cohesiveness.

Current Telephone Directory

Save your current white pages! You will be surprised how often you will need to refer to the old phone book, even months after you have relocated.

Memories

Take plenty of photos of the children with their friends, of your friends, of your home and favorite places. Compile a small album to leave out at the new house or make individual albums for each child. The photos will provide comfort while adjusting to the new surroundings. If you anticipate moving frequently, you may someday accumulate a collection of various home photo albums. Even years after the move, and/or subsequent moves, you will enjoy looking back fondly through the photographs. Think of them as a pictorial essay of the places you have lived.

Chapter 12

MOVING DAY

Here come the packers! Borrow a cooler and stock it with ice and drinks for the packers. These people are handling everything you own; you want them to enjoy doing so. Remind them to take a lunch break. If they did not bring their lunch, take orders for the fast food of your choice. Remember, people perform better when happy.

You will be amazed how swiftly every material possession is wrapped and loaded into a cardboard box of varying size. Young children can be particularly dismayed. A group of strangers have come into their home, are putting all its contents into boxes, and taking the boxes away. Sounds very close to the burglars that parents warn their children about. And to make matters worse, you are helping the thieves! "Are they going to give our stuff back?" is a question often posed, and children truly wonder. Explain the process, start to finish, and then remind them as packing day approaches. Even if the children will not be present for the packing end, they will certainly experience unpacking to some extent. They will wonder who loaded the boxes in the first place. Again, a little information goes a long way. By this time the fear of the unknown is piqued.

Each box is tagged with a number. The inventory sheet lists each number again and a corresponding brief description of the box's contents, i.e., "035 dishpack--glasses." Watching this can be very unsettling. I used to worry about my grandmother's wine glasses, the macaroni Christmas tree my daughter had made in preschool--items with sentimental value. Do not hesitate to point out these items to the movers, telling them of their value only to you. We have found they are more than happy to use extra wrapping to ensure the item's safe journey. (After all, they do get paid by the pound.) In the early moves I would try to either pack or transport sentimental items myself. After several disappointments I learned professional packers are much better than I am at doing their job. Imagine that!

Unfortunately, we have had some other disappointments as well. I caution you to keep a close eye on valuables. *Check that your valuable items are listed on the inventory sheet.* That way if items are lost or misplaced, at least you will have a record, and a replacement value can be assigned. Our toolbox was misplaced during one move; ironically, it was omitted from the inventory sheet as well.

Usually one person will start packing the kitchen while you walk around with the team leader. He will be inventorying the condition of the furniture, for example. Every scratch and dent will be noted, so only the new scratches and dents can be blamed on the move. Make sure his assessment is accurate. Also point out to him those inevitable items that are staying, like left over paint or the curtains you sold to the next owners. The movers will probably want you to group the items to be left behind in one area. You may want to do that ahead of time, or you may need the extra muscle to help you do that on packing day. Or tag the items remaining consistently and obviously, like with colorful ribbons.

Keep a marker handy. The movers do a good job of labeling which room the box was packed in, but if you would like to be more specific, write directly on the box. This makes unpacking smoother. You may also have items currently in the dining room that will be in the living room of the next house. You can indicate the room change yourself, since the packers will write the item's current room location. Write as much on these boxes as you need. Just keep in mind you simply cannot get to every box to label it before the move. The movers work quickly, and you are outnumbered.

Pack an "Open First" box of items you will want immediately--such as, toilet paper, soap, bed and bath linens, coffee maker and supplies, paper towels and the telephone. Ask the movers to place that box last on the truck, so it will be first off into your new home. Also pack a suitcase for everyone. You will need to provide for the evening after the movers leave with your household, the days required en route, and the first day at your new destination as well. Store these suitcases where they will not be loaded onto the truck, preferably at a neighbor's house.

The best advice I can lend is to stay calm and as

relaxed as possible. If you need to take a break, arrange for a neighbor to come in and help "look over the movers' shoulders" for a while. Keep in mind your possessions are merely material objects, and aside from sentimental value, everything can be replaced.

If the children are under foot, give them a job. Hand older ones a marker and ask them to write more details about the boxes' contents if possible. Occasionally the movers will "employ" a child for the day if he can really be helpful. Give smaller children a box to play in away from the main commotion. Little ones can entertain themselves for hours in a wardrobe box.

Once everything is packed up and securely placed inside the moving van, walk through the house. Check closets, attic and crawl space, garage, shed--everywhere that could be hiding overlooked items to be packed. Remember the outside planters and personalized mailbox too. You will be thoroughly exhausted by the end of the day. However you plan to spend your last evening in the area, you will probably want to make sure it's a short one.

Be prepared to provide the truck driver with precise directions to your new home from the nearest highway or freeway. Give him your new phone number, and plan to be there first. Ask what time they anticipate arriving and give instructions on how best to approach the house for unloading. Where do the movers plan to spend the night? Now that you have just entrusted them with your every possession, you have a right to know. Get phone numbers for the truck and the dispatcher in case you need to contact them along the way for any reason.

Chapter 13

BEFORE UNPACKING

Just because you have closed on the new house and taken possession, does not mean you must move in immediately. You may want to delay moving in order to allow for repairs, remodeling, or decorating. Sanding floors, cleaning carpets, painting, or remodeling a kitchen are all easier done in an empty home. If your time frame allows for time spent this way, I whole-heartedly recommend it. Depending on how long your project will take, you may want to spend your interim time in a suite hotel, a furnished "executive" apartment, or a rented house. If you are worried the movers will nick new paint or wallpaper, etc., they will usually repair any damage they create. Inquire about your mover's policy ahead of time.

If you are considering taking possession before you actually move into the house, plan accordingly with the movers. Most likely, you will need to delay packing your current home until you are ready to actually make the move. Once your household is on the truck, any delay in delivery becomes costly.

Storage--If you are planning to pack and load your items into storage for a while, special consideration must be taken. Plants rarely live on the truck, let alone in storage, so they must be moved separately if at all. Anything that is sensitive to temperature changes, such as a piano, needs to be stored separately in a heated space. Furniture that has recently been refinished cannot have items packed on top or against the fresh finish and will require individual attention. Ask your moving company representative to educate you on the subject of storage long before you choose this as an option. If you are planning to store some items and take the rest to a temporary home, label the boxes accordingly when they are packed.

Chapter 14

MOVING IN

Exciting! This is a high-energy day. The movers work quickly, you are in your new surroundings and eager to be settled again. Low level giggles can be heard all day. This day is hectic, so welcome all the help you can get. This day also commemorates the start of the family's next phase of life, so make sure the children are involved and part of the process. Every age can have a job. Young children can unpack toys, place books on shelves, "set up" their rooms. Older children can get settled into their own rooms and also help with community space like the family room.

With any luck new neighbors and children will stop by to meet you. Moving day has always provided for an exhilarating beginning. The next day, however, can feel completely different when you are exhausted and knee-deep in boxes throughout your house!

Usually the movers will ask the customers to man the inventory sheet. As the mover carries in a box and yells out its number, that number is found and checked off the sheet. Either my husband, my oldest, or I have done this while another of us directs movers to various rooms. The movers do not know which is the "play room," "baby's room," etc. Decide *before* the movers carry in the furniture where you would like it to be placed. They will set up the beds, so you need to decide where you want them.

Inspect the furniture for any damage, and bring anything in question to the attention of the group leader. You will have up to nine months to file a claim or a report on damaged goods. During that nine-month period you will have unpacked everything from off-season toys to holiday decorations. Be sure to obtain the necessary forms from the movers on moving day. Again, keep the movers happy and well supplied with food and drink that day as well. You want them to enjoy taking care of your possessions.

Try to unpack at least enough to make bedtime comfortable and getting showered and dressed in the morning effortless. Hopefully, these items are in your "open first" box. If there is time left over, get out into the neighborhood. Now that you live there, you may be viewing your new neighborhood through different eyes. A new phase of your family's adjustment begins now. Take out that smile and get off to a good start. The house will be unpacked eventually; now is the time to find some friends and get those roots beginning to sprout! The routine for our last move was to unpack boxes in the morning; play and explore our new area in the afternoon. Helped us make a lot of progress on both fronts.

Keep those change of address cards and stamps handy still. The post office for your former address will continue forwarding mail for a year. You will continue to notify people and companies of your new address, even if you have sent out holiday cards at Thanksgiving and change of address notices to everyone in your personal address book.

Chapter 15

_____

DON'T WAIT

We all want to feel comfortable and connected in our surroundings. How quickly this is accomplished is mainly *up to you.* Too often we wait for the "right time" to do anything that will help us feel settled in our new location and get caught up with "firsts"--First, I want to get fully unpacked; first, I want to decorate; first, someone needs to approach me; first, I need to get myself together . . . The longer you delay, the more difficult getting out there can become. And the children are taking your lead.

Take the initiative. Chances are really good your neighbors are very eager to know you but are hesitant to barge in. Think about how you regard a newcomer to your neighborhood. Are you hesitant because you do not know how they feel about moving there? Instead of waiting, invite your immediate neighbors over for dessert. Give them the opportunity to get to know you and your family instead of waiting for them to create that opportunity. Let them know how you are doing emotionally so they know how to approach you.

Do not waste time becoming acquainted with your neighbors. Tell them your children's ages and enlist their help finding playmates. A neighbor may even come equipped with a neighborhood directory. The sooner you and your family become acquainted with your neighbors, the sooner you will all begin to feel at home. A very active, social child will become grumpy very fast without playmates. Put him in a position to meet friends--quickly.

We have always lived too far from relatives for frequent visits, often too far to share holidays. Neighbors have become very important to us. I put people into three categories: family, friends, neighbors. If by chance any of those groups overlap, that is truly a blessing. We have learned to rely on our neighbors as family, especially in times of need, like when we were about to deliver our second child. If that neighbor we awakened at two AM was not as close as family before then, she surely was afterwards.

When family members cannot be present on a holiday, we fill the house with special neighbors who are in a similar situation. That neighborly bond becomes very special when given the chance. The children have surrogate cousins, aunts, and uncles. They will thrive on the atmosphere created with their special guests. So don't delay! Wonderful relationships are out there everywhere, just waiting for your "OK" to bloom.

At just about any time of year, you can find a reason to host a gathering for adults, your children, or both. If a combination party seems overwhelming, host a kids party and ask some parents you would like to get to know to stay and help.

We moved into a house once nearing the end of school,

and on the last day of school invited the neighborhood children over for an end-of-year barbecue. It was the easiest event. We cooked burgers and dogs, offered bags of chips and pretzels, a huge jar of pickles, and a cooler of soda. A few parents stayed, and we got to know each other in a very casual setting. The kids were delighted and proud to have their house as the gathering spot.

If you are not ready to have company, designate a meeting place--the park, roller rink, bowling alley, softball field. Ask the children and neighbors for ideas, and enlist their help in the planning.

If you do not have sufficient cause for celebration, create one. New neighbors hosted a surprise breakfast. We were awakened and prodded out of bed at seven AM by a neighbor in her pajamas, a mug of coffee in her fist, telling us to come as we were--NOW--to the neighbor's house for breakfast. Of course turnout was terrific. And somehow seeing everyone with p.j.'s and morning breath put us all on the same level. It was a wonderful way to begin a weekend, get to know our immediate neighbors, and start the day.

Shop around until you feel comfortable in a church or synagogue and join. Church "families" can provide much needed comfort when you are feeling far from "home." Increasingly, churches and synagogues offer programs for all age groups including sports, recreation, and classes on various topics. If you want the whole family to become involved in different branches of a unified base, a church or synagogue can provide the best opportunities with an added boost of support as well.

Many areas offer new-comers' groups for people moving into the area. These groups are often listed in the paper and are well worth looking into. You will meet people in your situation, and joining will expose you to places and people you could not begin to imagine because you are unfamiliar with the area. Some people use this type of group as a springboard to forming smaller, more intimate groups--such as, play groups, book clubs, etc.

My husband and I like to cook, and our favorite thing to do is entertain small groups for dinner. Wherever we go we organize a dinner club. We invite two or three couples to join, each couple provides a dish, and we alternate houses each time we meet. This group easily evolves into our core group of friends because we not only look forward to getting together, but rely on the consistency in our busy lives. This idea can easily be extended to families as well. This works well when the children are close in age, especially if the children become friends as well. But do not let varying age groups stop you either. Often this can work beautifully without the pressure for the kids to get along with their intended partners.

Chapter 16

REGARDING MOM AND DAD

You have perhaps the most difficult task of all: helping your children adjust. A family decision has uprooted you from your comfortable home, routine, and surroundings and landed you in a far away place, forced to start over again. And you wonder if you are up to the challenge. Realizing you are the glue that holds the family together, you make a commitment to pull your family through this adjustment with positive results.

When your new schedule precludes your being home as much as usual or when your new position preoccupies your mind, your spouse is called on to combat the tension that ensues. If your spouse is in a similar situation, special care must be devoted to maintaining domestic harmony. Broaden your shoulders to make room for not only the children but your spouse as well. "But *he/she* is the reason I'm in this situation!" you cry. Chances are good you are all in this situation to better your collective lives, so get over it. Everyone will need more comfort, and you will need to provide it for each other as well as the children. In the long run, you will be so glad you did.

This is why I whole-heartedly recommend that your spouse put off his/her job hunt until the family has adjusted reasonably well. You and your spouse made the decision to move for good reasons. Keep that in mind, even when the pressure is stacked against you. Your children will be watching your every reaction and emotion, taking their cues from you. If you resent your spouse for moving, you can bet they will too. If you wallow in self-pity when you feel you haven't a friend in the world, pick up the phone and call a friend. This may be all you need to bolster your confidence to find some local friends.

And if you put on a smile each day and announce your plans to "go get 'em" and appear exhilarated by the challenge, your children will too. Lead the way in approaching new friends, showing your children how to go about it, regardless of their ages. Remember you can learn from them as well. Being older does not make one better at approaching people. If your six-year-old is having no difficulty making friends, maybe everyone should sit back and "take notes."

My son and I are basically very shy. We were relatively new to a neighborhood and heard of a boy his age recently moving in a few blocks away. When I suggested we go ring his doorbell, he was surprised, to say the least, knowing how uncomfortable I would be as well as he. As we walked over I explained how we both need to get over our shyness, and how we could only benefit by welcoming this new family into the neighborhood. Needless to say, the boys became friends, the parents became friends, and my son and I became closer because we helped each other.

Take Time for Yourself

When children, a new location, and job change are involved, diving into anything else that requires your time can be disastrous. In addition to your everyday demands, your focus should be on easing your family's adjustment, staying on top of schoolwork, and doing whatever seems necessary to get your family's home life in order and running smoothly again. Once that is accomplished, you can slowly peruse your options and take it from there.

In the meantime, however, I strongly recommended you find one outlet that is strictly your own from the beginning. Get involved in one group or activity you really enjoy and become as involved as you comfortably can. For instance, join a sports team, a book club, take a class, seek out your college alumni club--something for your own enjoyment that gets you out of the house, away from the office, and with people who share similar interests. Even if you simply have coffee with a friend Saturday mornings, do something for yourself. You will find all the giving you do comes a bit more easily when you take something for yourself as well.

The Inevitable

No matter how well you plan or are prepared emotionally, the blues will strike to some degree. They may be triggered by the pang experienced when you realize you are lost while driving; the lonely, sinking feeling on Sunday night, noticing the phone has not rung all weekend; or worst of all when you discover your child hiding face down on his bed sobbing for the friends he has left behind. (And even if he has made a lot of new friends, more than likely at some point he will long for the old, more comfortable relationships.) You have all been stripped of your comforts, and you need to find new ones.

The comfort zone returns usually within the first year, so hang in there in the interim. How long that period drags on is completely up to you. Getting out there and making friends is so important for each family member. Friends are waiting in the neighborhood, school, work, church, everywhere. *Put yourself in the position to meet them.*

But no matter how well that plastered smile fits, at some point it will come off, and you will experience meltdown. The key is paving the way for friendships *before* this occurs. Our last move was perhaps my easiest because I was fully prepared, and my plastered smile fit so well I rarely took it off. Until one Sunday afternoon I fell apart. My poor husband didn't know how to comfort me. I explained to him that I felt I was following all the aforementioned advice, and still I felt like an outsider. Nearing the end of a good cry, which felt great by the way, the phone rang. It was a friend we had made through the office calling to invite us to a dinner party. She was planning a fun gathering and was eager for us to meet their friends. Needless to say my tears dried immediately!

"Getting yourself out there" does take a lot of effort and energy, but the rewards are limitless. Challenge your confidence and stamina. After all, we are all just people with similar needs for friendships. So do what you do best, and become someone's friend.

Sometimes the blues are too difficult to shake with mere perseverance. If this is the case, try some or all of the following to boost your spirits:

1. Volunteer in a situation where people are more needy than yourself. Work the soup kitchen, cuddle babies confined to the hospital, help out at the nursing home--there are many opportunities to help. Lighten someone else's load, and in so doing, lighten your own. At the same time, you are setting a great example for your children too. They can become involved in many volunteer efforts as well. People confined to nursing homes benefit from visitors of any age, infants to adult.

2. Exercise! Exercise is a wonderful way to clear the mind and rejuvenate the body. Strike an exercise level that leaves you invigorated rather than completely exhausted. Try briskly walking throughout your new neighborhood. Go to the Y before work or at lunchtime. Join exercise classes and make friends as well.

3. Another way to ward off the blues is to surround yourself with beautiful things. Roam the art museum, visit the art galleries, drive through a beautiful park. Invite a potential friend or two along and make it a great day. Have lunch outside.

4. Completing a project can help. Organize that photo album or closet. Stick to projects that are easily accomplished in a relatively short period of time when you need a lift. A stressful, tedious project may only worsen your state of mind. Close to immediate satisfaction is a good goal to set.

Keep in mind that experiencing the blues is normal, expected, and will pass. As with any new situation, give yourself a year to adjust. You can only be pleasantly surprised if you try.

Chapter 17

NECESSITIES

Finding Your Way

Equip each car and the house with an updated street map. The bookstores usually sell laminated maps that fold nicely to fit into small places. If not, ask your Realtor or AAA for some. Familiarize yourself with names of main thoroughfares, trace your way to the hospital, post office, airport, mall, etc. Keep your map handy and refer to it whenever taking directions. You need know only where *you* are on the map; the person responding from your destination will get you wherever you want to be.

For instance, you want to redecorate, and you would like to look at paint chips. Call the number you found for the paint store from the yellow pages, tell them where you are and let them direct you. If you are just too far, ask if they have a branch closer to you and that phone number.

When the children need a ride anywhere, call ahead for directions. Keep a small notebook with an inside pocket in your car just for directions. Use the pocket to store the directions you have taken when the notebook was not handy. You can use the notebook to take directions when you are out. For example, if you are at a store, and they suggest you see their branch location, write the directions in your notebook, and you will have them for future reference. Write the phone numbers for your destinations as well just in case you do get lost.

When your child is invited to play at a friend's, you will need to ask directions only once. Volunteer to drive for field trips. That will force you into the area, but the added bonus is having someone to follow. Before long you will have that behind-the-wheel confidence again, impressing your family and yourself as well.

Choosing a Dentist

Finding a dentist is such a personal decision, but visiting your dentist just before you leave allows most people six months in which to find a new one. Ask neighbors and acquaintances for recommendations. Usually if you ask enough people, you will notice recommendations being repeated. That's a great start. If after you go you are not happy, you have another six months to find someone else.

Choosing an OB-GYN

We moved when I was eight months pregnant, so finding a trusted OB quickly was essential. I did not have time to ask around for recommendations. I called the closest hospital and spoke to the head nurse in Labor and Delivery. I explained my situation and asked her whom she would recommend. Prepared for the "I can't give out that kind of information" line, I first had circled in the yellow pages all the OBs in my area. Explaining again just how far along I was, I pleaded with her for a verbal thumbs up as I read off the list. Taking her most emphatic "u-huh," I found a wonderful doctor and had a very positive experience as a result. Now this approach may not work every time, but keep in mind there are three shifts for each day. Someone is bound to be helpful.

The very quality that turns off a friend may be a reason you would like that particular doctor. For instance a friend had recommended a practice of three doctors but told me to avoid one in particular because he was old, although very well respected. I prefer an older, fatherly type with years of experience to a young, handsome, blushing GYN any day! Her word of caution turned into my valued recommendation.

Finding a Pediatrician or Family Doctor

We have had best results going with doctors recommended by friends and neighbors. The best bet is to choose a group of doctors; then you can narrow your choice down to one favorite from there. Preschool physicals and sports physicals are good tools for evaluating a doctor.

You can also set appointments to merely interview doctors. In fact, that's encouraged. Take your children with you to get their reactions and opinions as well. They are the ones who will, most likely, be seeing the doctor. You can talk about the practice, what insurance they take, the general philosophy of the doctors in that practice. This gives you the opportunity to comfortably choose a doctor or practice *before* your youngest spikes a fever of 104 degrees. If you find a doctor affiliated with a group of doctors, you are always certain someone will be available when you are in need.

Finding a Hair Stylist

Easy! Great haircuts are everywhere, just look around wherever you go. When you see one you like, compliment the cut and ask where he/she goes and take it from there.

Services

Finding services such as dry cleaners and repairmen may take a little longer to find and may require some trial and error. Rule of thumb for repairmen: Get three estimates, and convince the one you like the most to do the job for the best price. Everything is negotiable. Just knowing who to call in every situation is very comforting. And always ask for references.

Decorating

This can prove to be the best way to help you make friends while you finish your home. Ask around for advice on where to go for fabric, furniture, and the like, ask an acquaintance to accompany you and make a day of it. When you see a home that is decorated to your taste, ask if they had help. If not, ask for *their* help. People are usually willing to help if the favor is prefaced by a compliment.

Chapter 18

HIGHLIGHT THE BENEFITS

One of the definitions offered in Webster's Dictionary for change is: to undergo transformation, transition, or substitution. Change is good. Change forces us to exceed our self-imposed limitations, and the benefits can be limitless. By relocating we are given the chance to start again, to try new approaches to life, to begin with a clean slate, a chance to become more self-reliant individually and as a family.

Have you ever looked back on an antic you had done in your youth and gotten away with and thought, "Am I glad I did that then because I would never have the guts to do that now."? This is a similar opportunity. Make a move now. Hopefully, you will look back on this time with that same admiration, glad you "went for it" when you had the chance. Life is to be enjoyed--make the most of it!

One of the benefits of moving is making friends in far reaching places and keeping them. The best way your child can realize this as an advantage is by your example. Make the effort to keep in touch by dropping small notes or e-mail and an occasional phone call. Write round-robin letters to families you have left behind. Everyone can write a portion, however long or brief, of one letter. Think of it as a family project to brighten someone's day. My youngest could not write when we moved last, so she drew pictures, and I wrote what she wanted to say.

Put the emphasis on the actual effort to keep in touch rather than on receiving a response. Disappointment can then be downplayed if a timely response is not forthcoming. Focus on the fun you have together and the impact you will create for the recipient.

Moving can strengthen a family. You rely on each other for fun and friendship and can develop a strong bond as a result. Exploring an area together, learning from each other, sharing your new experiences--the whole relocating process can bring a family closer if faced in a unified, positive way. Focus on the good; develop the strengths.

Remember, throughout this adjustment period children will look to you, Mom and Dad, for guidance. If you continue to mope about friends you have left, they will too. Togetherness is the key. Discuss your feelings and emphasize the positive. View the move as a challenge, a chance to test yourself, to grow as an individual and as a family. Sibling relationships can grow stronger; family ties, deeper. Mom and Dad, you set the tone. Keep that plastered smile handy, in fact, put it on every morning. Spoon out the encouragement each morning at breakfast and accolades at dinner. Just know the children are watching you very closely, so give them the best performance you can offer. Continue this attitude long after you have moved as well. Eventually, it may just come naturally.

I feel very fortunate to have moved as often as we have.

While I often insist I would like to stay put for a while; the sight of a moving van causes excitement to well up inside me. I wonder where they are off to, what new adventures they will experience, how life will change in the most unexpected ways. I admire people who have the guts to keep on going, keep on experiencing. And what better way to experience a place than to live there? I hope my children develop this enthusiasm for moving or at least do not close their eyes to it. Moving provides an added dimension to life. And besides, someday we will be too old to keep on moving. We will then have to settle for visiting our children.

NOTES

NOTES

NOTES

NOTES

NOTES

NOTES

ORDER FORM

To order your copy of <u>Smooth Moves</u> directly from the publisher, fill out the following information, enclose your check or money order, and mail to:

Teacup Press
Post Office Box 21212
Charlotte, NC 28277

Name: _____

Address: _____

City: _____ State: _____ Zip: _____

Telephone: (___) _____

Sales Tax:
Add 7% for books shipped to North Carolina addresses.

Shipping and Handling: Included.

Payment:
Please enclose your personal check or money order.

Delivery:
Please allow two to three weeks for delivery.

ORDER FORM

To order your copy of <u>Smooth Moves</u> directly from the publisher, fill out the following information, enclose your check or money order, and mail to:

Teacup Press
Post Office Box 21212
Charlotte, NC 27277

Name: _____

Address: _____

City: _____ State: ___ Zip: _____

Telephone: (___)_____

Sales Tax:
Add 7% for books shipped to North Carolina addresses.

Shipping and Handling: Included.

Payment:
Please enclose your personal check or money order.

Delivery:
Please allow two to three weeks for delivery.